ACCORDION
POLKA FAVORITES

ARRANGED BY
KENNY KOTWITZ

CONTENTS

ISBN 978-0-7935-1479-3

HAL•LEONARD®
CORPORATION
7777 W. BLUEMOUND RD. P.O. BOX 13819 MILWAUKEE, WI 53213

Beer Barrel Polka
(Roll Out The Barrel)
Based on the European success "SKODA LASKY"*

By Lew Brown, Wladimir A. Timm,
Jaromir Vejvoda and Vasek Zeman

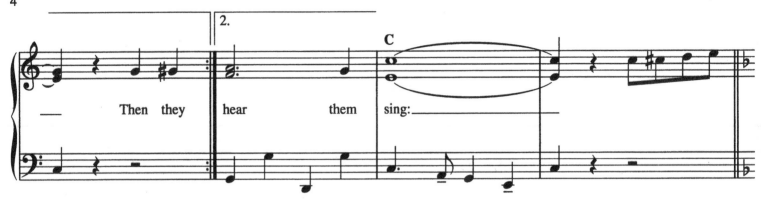

Then they hear them sing:

Roll out the bar - rel,

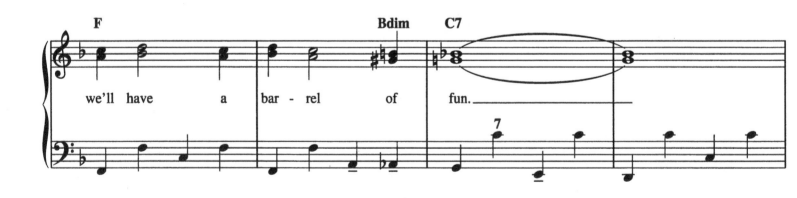

we'll have a bar - rel of fun.

Roll out the bar - rel,

Crying Polka

By Frank Loesser
and Milton DeLugg

Emilia Polka

Lyric by Albert Gamse
Music by Walter Dana

The Happy Wanderer

Words by Antonia Ridge
Music by Friedrich W. Moller

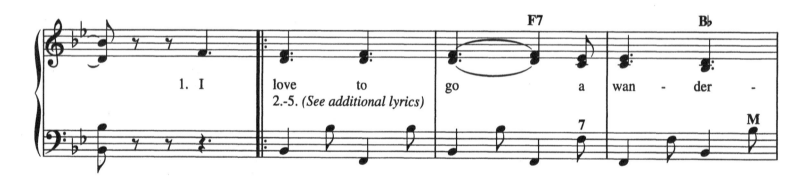

Additional Lyrics

2. I love to wander by the stream that dances in the sun.
   So joyously it calls to me, "Come! join my happy song!"
   Val-de-ri, Val-de-ra, Val-de-ra, Val-de ha ha ha ha ha ha
   Val-de-ri, Val-de-ra, "Come! join my happy song!"

3. I wave my hat to all I meet, and they wave back to me.
   And black birds call so loud and sweet from ev'ry greenwood tree.
   Val-de-ri, Val-de-ra, Val-de-ra, Val-de ha ha ha ha ha ha
   Val-de-ri, Val-de-ra, from ev'ry greenwood tree.

4. High overhead, the skylarks wing, they never rest at home.
   But just like me, they love to sing, as o'er the world we roam.
   Val-de-ri, Val-de-ra, Val-de-ra, Val-de ha ha ha ha ha ha
   Val-de-ri, Val-de-ra, as o'er the world we roam.

5. Oh, may I go a wandering until the day I die!
   Oh, may I always laugh and sing, beneath God's clear blue sky!
   Val-de-ri, Val-de-ra, Val-de-ra, Val-de ha ha ha ha ha ha
   Val-de-ri, Val-de-ra, beneath God's clear blue sky!

Hoop-Dee-Doo

Words by Frank Loesser
Music by Milton DeLugg

Lyrics:
Hoop - dee - doo, hoop - dee - doo,
I hear a pol - ka and my trou - bles are through.
Hoop - dee - doo, hoop - dee - dee,

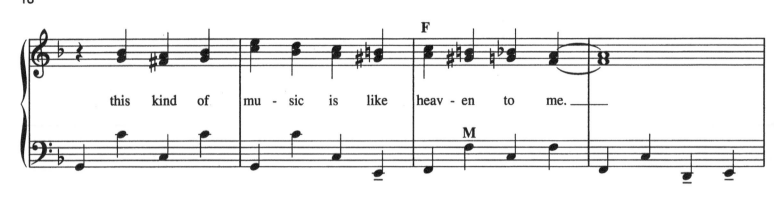

this kind of mu - sic is like heav - en to me.

Hoop - dee - doo,   hoop - dee - doo,

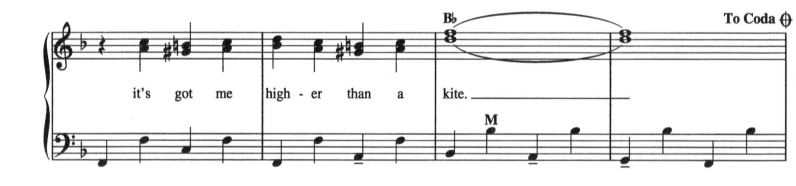

it's got me high - er than a   kite.   **To Coda** ⊕

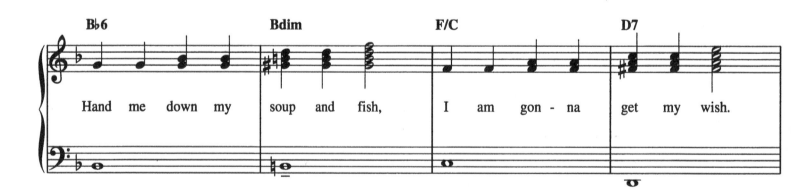

Bb6   **Bdim**   **F/C**   **D7**

Hand me down my   soup and fish,   I am gon - na   get my wish.

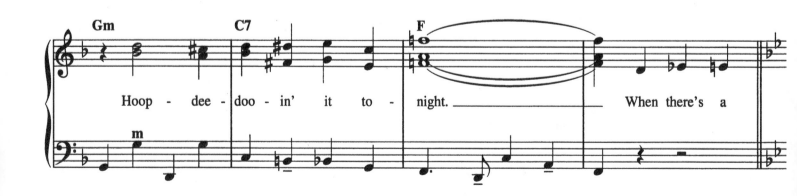

Gm   **C7**   **F**

Hoop - dee - doo - in' it to - night.   When there's a

21

Hop-Scotch Polka

Words and Music by Carl Sigman,
Gene Rayburn and William Whitlock

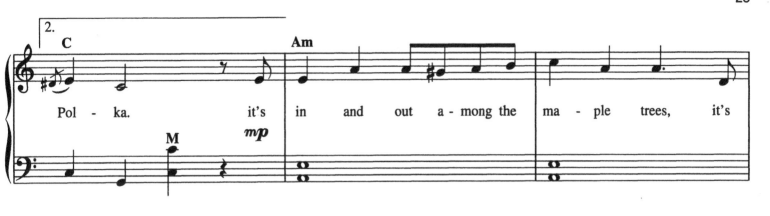

Pol - ka. it's in and out a - mong the ma - ple trees, it's

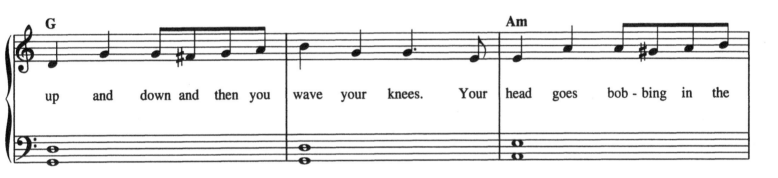

up and down and then you wave your knees. Your head goes bob - bing in the

morn - ing breeze to the Hop - Scotch Pol - ka. Oh, you

hop a lit - tle on your lit - tle left shoe, you

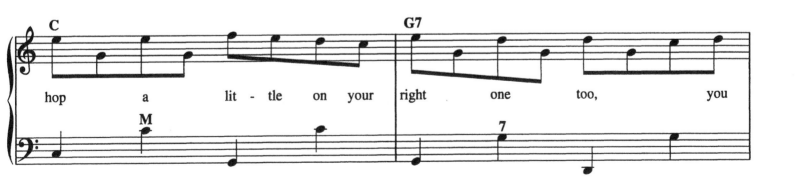

hop a lit - tle on your right one too, you

24

Just Another Polka

Words and Music by Frank Loesser
and Milton DeLugg

Jolly Peter

By John A. Bassett,
M. Werner-Kersten

With a bounce

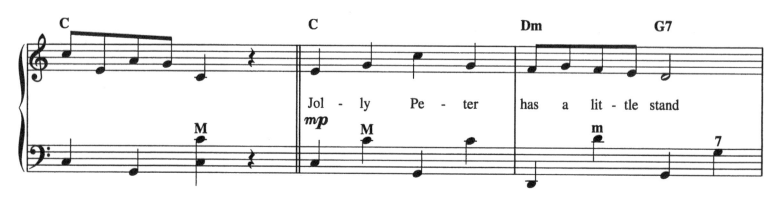

Jol - ly Pe - ter has a lit - tle stand

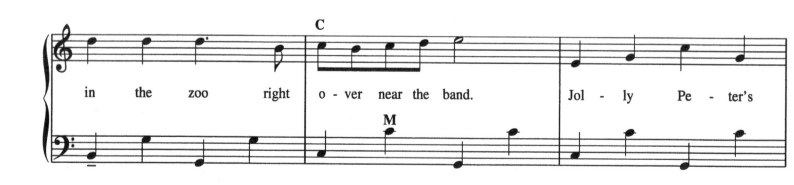

in the zoo right o - ver near the band. Jol - ly Pe - ter's

al - ways in the park where he's hap - py as a lark. Ev - 'ry day that's

31

Just Because

Words and Music by Bob and Joe Shelton
and Sid Robin

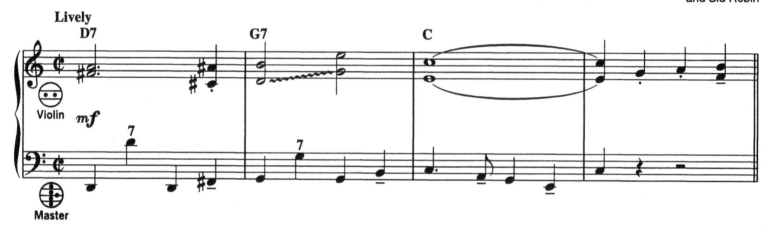

Just be-cause you think you're so pret-ty

just be-cause you think you're so hot,

just be-cause you think you've got some-thing, that no-bod-y

Liechtensteiner Polka

Words and Music by Ed Kotscher
and R. Lindt

Boldly and precise

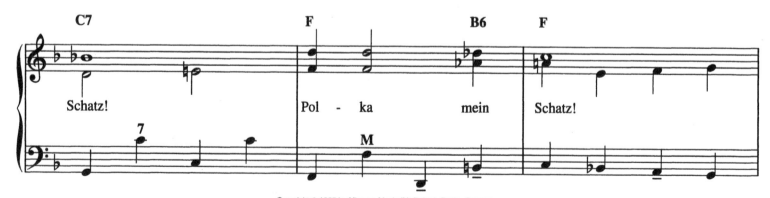

so ei - ne Liech - ten - stei - ner pol - ka die

hat's, die macht Ra - batz. Mein

Schatz!

Der al - te Herr von Liech - ten - stein,

Ja! Ja! Ja! Der konn - te nicht al - lei - ne sein.

The Merry Christmas Polka

Words by Paul Francis Webster
Music by Sonny Burke

They're tun - ing up the fid - dles now, the fid - dles now, the fid - dles now. There's wine to warm the mid - dles now and set your head a - whirl. A -

42

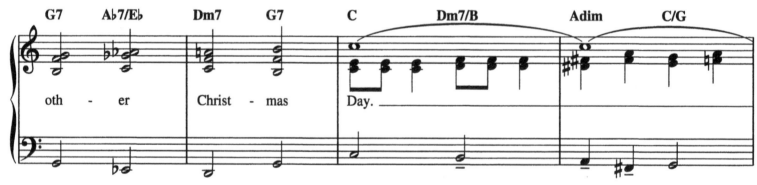

B♭ F
one be hap - py and gay.
la - dy step with her beau.
M M
B♭ C7
Oh, it's the time to be jol - ly and
A - round a tree to the ceil - ing with
M 7
F C7 Dm Gm
deck the halls with hol - ly. So let's have a
lots of time for steal - ing those kiss - es be -
M 7 m m
Am B♭6 Bm7♭5 C D♭7 C7
jol - ly hol - i - day! Come on and
neath the mis - tle - toe! Come on and
F
dance the Mer - ry Christ - mas Pol - ka.
dance the Mer - ry Christ - mas Pol - ka.
M

44

My Melody Of Love

English and Polish Lyrics by Bobby Vinton
German Lyrics by George Buschor
Music by Henry Mayer

Paloma Blanca

Words and Music by
Hans Bouwens

Pennsylvania Polka

By Lester Lee
and Zeke Manners

Tic-Tock Polka

Lyric by S. Guski and R.J. Martino
Music by G. Lama

Too Fat Polka
(She's Too Fat For Me)

By Ross MacLean
and Arthur Richardson

HAL·LEONARD
ACCORDION
PLAY·ALONG

The Accordion Play-Along series features custom accordion arrangements with CD tracks recorded by a live band (accordion, bass and drums). There are two audio tracks for each song – a full performance for listening, plus a separate backing track which lets you be the soloist! The CD is playable on any CD player, and is also enhanced so Mac and PC users can adjust the recording to any tempo without changing the pitch!

1. POLKA FAVORITES
arr. Gary Meisner

Beer Barrel Polka (Roll Out the Barrel) • Hoop-Dee-Doo • Hop-scotch Polka • Just Another Polka • Just Because • Pennsylvania Polka • Tic-Tock Polka • Too Fat Polka (She's Too Fat for Me).
00701705 Book/CD Pack...$19.99

2. ALL-TIME HITS
arr. Gary Meisner

Edelweiss • Fly Me to the Moon (In Other Words) • I Left My Heart in San Francisco • It's a Small World • Moon River • More (Ti Guarderò Nel Cuore) • Poinciana (Song of the Tree) • When I'm Sixty-Four.
00701706 Book/CD Pack...$19.99

3. CLASSIC SONGS
arr. Gary Meisner

Carnival of Venice • Ciribiribin • Come Back to Sorrento • Fascination (Valse Tzigane) • Funiculi, Funicula • I Love You Truly • In the Good Old Summertime • Melody of Love • Peg O' My Heart • When Irish Eyes Are Smiling.
00701707 Book/CD Pack...$14.99

4. CHRISTMAS SONGS
arr. Gary Meisner

Frosty the Snow Man • Have Yourself a Merry Little Christmas • Here Comes Santa Claus (Right down Santa Claus Lane) • The Most Wonderful Time of the Year • Rudolph the Red-Nosed Reindeer • Santa Claus Is Comin' to Town • Silver Bells • Winter Wonderland.
00101770 Book/CD Pack...$14.99

5. ITALIAN SONGS
arr. Gary Meisner

La Sorella • La Spagnola • Mattinata • 'O Sole Mio • Oh Marie • Santa Lucia • Tarantella • Vieni Sul Mar.
00101771 Book/CD Pack...$14.99

HAL·LEONARD®

Visit Hal Leonard online at **www.halleonard.com**